ANTIGUA
TRAVEL GUIDE
2024

**The Complete Handbook to Exploring
Antigua's Beautiful Sights, History, Food, and
Culture.**

JACK MILIGAN

TABLE OF CONTENTS

TABLE OF CONTENTS...3

INTRODUCTION...5

   Brief History of Antigua.....................................7

CHAPTER ONE..10

   Selecting the Best Time to Visit Antigua.................10

   Visa and Entry Requirements................................12

   Currency and Budgeting.....................................15

CHAPTER TWO..19

   Air Travel Option..19

   Cruise Travel Option...22

   Local Transportation...25

CHAPTER THREE...29

   Antigua's Hotel Options....................................29

   Antigua's Resorts Options.................................32

   Vacation Rentals for Tailored Getaways.................36

   Popular Areas to Stay.......................................39

CHAPTER FOUR..44

   A Tour through Historical Sites...........................44

   The Natural Wonders of Antigua.........................48

   Antigua's Cultural Events..................................52

CHAPTER FIVE...57

   An Overview of the Island's Stunning Beaches......57

   Antigua's Water Sports.....................................61

Antigua Hiking Experiences....................................65

CHAPTER SIX.. **70**

Antigua Local Cuisine Experiences....................... 70

Antigua's Popular Restaurants and Cafés..............74

Dietary Considerations.. 79

CHAPTER SEVEN... **84**

Antigua's Local Markets..84

Handmade Items and Souvenirs........................... 88

Antigua's Duty-Free Shopping Extravaganza........93

CHAPTER EIGHT.. **98**

Bars and Nightclubs..98

Cultural Performances of Antigua........................ 102

CHAPTER NINE..**107**

Health and Safety... 107

Communication.. 111

Local Etiquette.. 115

CONCLUSION... **120**

INTRODUCTION

Greetings from the lovely island of Antigua, where lively culture and history coexist with sandy beaches. Located in the center of the Caribbean, Antigua entices travelers with its crystal-clear seas, powder-soft beaches, and magnetic charm.

Explore the ageless beauty and distinctive charms that make Antigua a gem of the Caribbean archipelago with the help of this travel guide. Take in everything of the island's fascinating history, from the English Harbour's colonial beauty to the abandoned sugar plantations that dot the countryside and each tells a story of a bygone period.

Antigua is a playground for adventure seekers as well as a tropical paradise. Hike through verdant jungles, explore coral reefs filled with marine life, or just unwind on immaculate beaches with the soothing sound of the waves serving as your soundtrack. Every facet of life on the island is infused with vivid culture, from the upbeat calypso rhythms to the flamboyant festivals honoring Antigua's rich cultural past.

Savor a gastronomic adventure that reflects the variety of the island, ranging from seafood specialties to fusion meals with Caribbean influences. Antigua comes alive at dusk with a vibrant nightlife that beckons you to dance beneath the stars or spend a peaceful evening by the waterfront.

This book is your key to discovering Antigua's hidden treasures; it offers advice on how to have an amazing trip, where to stay, and what to look for. Antigua welcomes you with open arms whether you're looking for an adventurous getaway or some downtime on the sandy shoreline. Prepare yourself for an experience that will leave you with memories fit for a postcard and a sense of Antigua that will stay with you long after you have left the island.

Brief History of Antigua

Antigua is a sparkling gem in the Caribbean Sea with a fascinating history that turns the pages like a well-read book. This island has seen decades of change, resiliency, and cultural fusion, from the native Arawak people to the colonial influences that defined its character.

The Arawak people inhabited Antigua for a very long time before European ships appeared in the distance. Archaeological site ruins provide witness to an old relationship between humans and the island's verdant surroundings, as evidenced by their presence. The Arawaks were expert farmers who turned the rich soil into a thriving community supported by the Caribbean's abundance.

Christopher Columbus initially passed the coast of Antigua in 1493, marking the beginning of the island's colonial history. Still, the English did not create the first European colony on the island until 1632. Taking its name from the Spanish saint Santa Maria de la Antigua, the English-influenced area set the stage for centuries of blending cultures.

Because of its advantageous position, the island was sought after in European power conflicts. It was owned by the French, the Spanish, and the Dutch until ending up as a British colony in 1667. During this time, Antigua's primary resource was its sugar plantations, which employed a significant number of African slaves who had been brought to the island as slaves.

The Antiguan sugar industry peaked in the 18th century. With its vast plantations dominating the terrain, the island became an essential part of the economic machinery of the British Empire. Relics from these sugar estates, such as Shirley Heights and Betty's Hope, serve as moving memories of this turbulent time in history.

Antigua saw a tremendous transformation in 1834 with the abolition of slavery. As the island's economy shifted to one with greater diversity, the freed populace had to confront the difficulties of creating a new community. The cultural fabric of Antigua, where customs from the Caribbean, Europe, and Africa combine to establish a singular identity, bears the echoes of this change.

Antigua experienced efforts toward self-governance as the 20th century concluded, and independence was finally attained in 1981. Today's bustling contemporary life coexists with proud cultural heritage and ruins of colonial architecture.

Through historical landmarks, museums, and forts, visitors to Antigua may learn more about the island's past and get a greater knowledge of its evolution over time. Beyond the sands of its stunning beaches, Antigua's history is woven into the very fabric of its people and its surroundings, telling a riveting story that envelops the visitor.

CHAPTER ONE

Selecting the Best Time to Visit Antigua

Choosing the best time to visit Antigua is like arranging a symphony of events, weather, and personal tastes; every note adds to the harmonic melody of the ultimate Caribbean getaway. Antigua warmly welcomes you all year round, whether you're looking for warm breezes, joyous festivities, or peaceful times. When is the ideal season to enjoy this paradise in the tropics?

December to April
The peak season in Antigua, which runs from December to April, is the epitome of picture-perfect weather. Take advantage of the pleasant weather, with highs of 75–85°F (24–29°C). Water lovers are drawn to the blue sky and pristine waterways for sailing, snorkeling, and lazy beach days. Plan to reserve the greatest lodgings and activities because this season also happens to be the busiest travel season on the island.

May to November

The summer and fall months, from May to November, mark the beginning of what the locals affectionately refer to as "Mango Season." Although this is the Caribbean hurricane season, there is little chance that Antigua will be directly impacted. On the other hand, anticipate seldom cool rainfall, verdant surroundings, and a calmer environment. For tourists on a tight budget who want to experience Antigua's charms without the crowds, now is the perfect time to go. Take advantage of occasions like the Antigua Charter Yacht Show in December or Carnival in July to immerse yourself in the island's colorful culture.

Festivals & Events

It might be a fantastic experience for those who are keen to fully immerse themselves in Antigua's vibrant culture to schedule their vacation around festivals. With its colorful parades and exuberant celebrations, the July carnival highlights the island's rich history. An exciting environment is created along the shore during the Antigua Sailing Week in April, which draws sailors from all over the world.

The ideal time to travel to Antigua ultimately depends on your priorities and tastes. Every month in Antigua's calendar tells a different narrative, whether it's the sun-drenched appeal of high season or the cozy charm of

Mango Season. You're invited to pen your own remarkable story on this Caribbean canvas.

Visa and Entry Requirements

Setting out for Antigua, the jewel of the Caribbean, needs some preparatory effort to guarantee a smooth arrival in this tropical paradise. Once you know the admission and visa procedures, it's like opening the door to paradise and you can concentrate on the blue seas and white sand beaches that lie ahead.

Visa Exemption
The good news for a lot of people is that citizens of many different nations are not required to get a visa to enter Antigua & Barbuda. Visas are not required for visits to Antigua for up to 90 days for nationals of the US, Canada, the UK, and the majority of EU member states. This kind of regulation makes it easier for a wide range of tourists to enjoy the island's natural beauty.

Entry Documents
Many tourists may not need a visa, however, there are a few mandatory entrance documents that cannot be waived. Make sure your passport is up to date and valid for at least six months beyond the day you want to travel. A multi-entry visa may be required if your trip involves

stops at other Caribbean islands, and the passport should have enough blank pages for stamps.

Long Stays and Unique Situations
There are other criteria if you want to remain longer or if you want to work or study in Antigua. Longer visits might call for a visa, and depending on the purpose and length of your stay, you might need to bring certain entry papers. It is best to check the official government website or get in touch with the closest Antiguan consulate for specific information relevant to your situation.

Health Safety Measures
Global health issues are becoming a crucial factor when organizing a trip. Although immunizations have not historically been required for admission into Antigua, it is advisable to be aware of any changes to any health-related regulations, particularly in light of the rapidly changing global environment. To make sure you follow any current health procedures, check with your healthcare professional and the appropriate health authorities.

Smooth Arrival Process
As the main entry point, Antigua's V.C. Bird International Airport guarantees a seamless arrival experience for guests. The procedures for customs and

immigration are usually simple, and the staff members are eager to greet you when you arrive on the island. To speed up your admission, make sure you have all the necessary paperwork readily available.

Beyond its stunning scenery, Antigua is known for its warm friendliness, which makes the immigration procedure just as fascinating as the island itself. A visa-free breeze greets you with a prepared set of paperwork, welcoming you to enter Antigua's warm embrace with open arms and a heart eager to welcome paradise.

Currency and Budgeting

The soft flutter of palm leaves greets you as soon as you step into Antigua's sun-drenched coastline. This Caribbean paradise is where the island's distinct identity is reflected in the currency. Comprehending the local currency and grasping budgetary guidelines is similar to interpreting a treasure map, guaranteeing that your visit is not only enlightening but economical as well.

East Caribbean Currency (XCD)
The East Caribbean Dollar (XCD) is Antigua and Barbuda's national currency. Even though the US dollar is commonly recognized and utilized in tourist

destinations, it is helpful to have some East Caribbean Dollars on hand for making purchases in smaller towns, local markets, and more isolated locations. Learn about the current exchange rate so that you can plan your stay and make wise selections.

Credit Cards

In most bigger facilities, including restaurants and hotels, credit cards are accepted. However, it's advisable to have extra cash on hand for smaller markets and sellers. To prevent any possible problems with card transactions, let your bank know when you will be traveling and find out whether there are any international transaction fees.

Cash

Local markets and smaller enterprises often prefer cash transactions, while resort regions could accommodate electronic purchases. You may move between the US and the Caribbean with ease if you have a combination of US and Caribbean currency. Major cities and popular tourist destinations have ATMs, which offer a practical means to withdraw local cash.

Managing Price Ranges

Like any location, Antigua has a range of activities to suit different price points. You have the option to customize your stay to fit within your budget, choosing from upscale resorts to quaint guesthouses and neighborhood restaurants. Visiting tiny, family-run restaurants and perusing local markets for mementos may provide a genuine experience without breaking the wallet.

Culinary Highlights with Regional Tastes
The cuisine of Antigua is a delicious fusion of Caribbean and foreign influences. Local eateries are what give the island its character, even though upmarket places may be more expensive. A fair way to experience the real flavor of Antigua is to indulge in robust indigenous meals or enjoy freshly caught seafood at a beachside shack.

Take Part in Local Culture at No Cost
Accept Antigua's colorful culture without breaking the bank. Enjoy free or inexpensive admission to historical places, go to local activities, and relax on immaculate beaches. Take in all of the island's rhythms, from the upbeat calypso beat to the vibrant celebrations of regional festivals.

With its turquoise seas and golden beaches, Antigua entices visitors with a diverse range of adventures. Equipped with knowledge of the local currency and astute financial advice, your trip through this paradisiacal Caribbean destination becomes not only unforgettable but also a showcase for the skill of thoughtful discovery.

CHAPTER TWO

Air Travel Option

As you daydream of Antigua's bright beaches and lush surroundings, the first step in your journey is to choose the best airline choice to take you to this Caribbean paradise. The well-connected airways of Antigua guarantee a smooth transition from the airport to the island's captivating coastlines, regardless of your preference for direct flights or a more picturesque route.

V.C. Bird International Airport
V.C. Bird International Airport, which is the main entry point into Antigua, bears the name of the first prime minister of the island. This contemporary airport, which connects the island to important cities in North America, Europe, and the Caribbean, welcomes a multitude of international flights and is only a short drive from St. John's, the capital. There are hubs in Miami, New York, London, Toronto, and other locations offering direct flights.

Connecting Flights
Connecting flights can provide extra possibilities for those looking to explore many destinations or those planning a multi-destination trip. Before arriving in Antigua, many tourists find it advantageous to pass

through important cities like Miami, Atlanta, or San Juan. This gives you options when selecting an airline and lets you stop and explore other places along the way.

Private Aircraft and Charter Flights
Private planes and charter flights appeal to individuals who value a customized travel experience and offer a hint of exclusivity. Private planes may land at Antigua's airport, offering an opulent and quick way to reach the island. Moreover, chartering a flight allows you to visit isolated Caribbean islands or neighboring islands.

Flight and Cruise Combos
If you want a fully immersed experience, think about adding a cruise to your trip. The ease of a cruise and the peace of a longer stay on the island may be combined with certain cruise lines' package deals that include airfare to Antigua.

Ground Transportation from the Airport
There are several ground transportation choices available to get you to your destination after you land in Antigua. There are plenty of taxis, rental vehicles, and airport shuttles to make the move from air to ground easy.

Attention to Seasons
Although Antigua is a year-round travel destination, it's important to take into account the seasonality of airline

availability and costs. High season, which runs from December to April, may see a spike in demand that affects the cost of tickets and lodging. On the other hand, shoulder seasons could provide better deals and a more relaxed attitude.

Antigua's warm embrace welcomes you as you take off on an aerial voyage. Whether you choose to take a connecting flight to broaden your travel options or go direct to save time, every time you land in Antigua, you can be sure that you're entering the magical Caribbean. So extend your wings and let your voyage to this alluring island getaway be driven by the hope of bliss.

Cruise Travel Option

A cruise to Antigua is an adventure that showcases the beauty of the Caribbean with each passing wave. It's more than simply a trip. Cruise alternatives abound, providing guests with an immersive and picturesque approach to this tropical paradise, ranging from opulent liners to tiny sailboats.

Cruise Liners
Several elite cruise ships choose Antigua as a port of call, which elevates your nautical experience. Antigua is included in the itineraries of well-known cruise lines like

Royal Caribbean, Celebrity Cruises, and Norwegian Cruise Line, enabling guests to take in the island's natural beauty while savoring the comforts and entertainment provided on board.

Sailing Cruises

Sailing cruises provide a different viewpoint for individuals who would like to have a more private and tranquil experience. Smaller sailing boats and catamarans ply the azure seas around Antigua, providing a more intimate relationship with the ocean and the liberty to discover quiet beaches and bays. For those who are passionate about sailing, some cruises even provide you the opportunity to try your hand at sailing.

Adventures on Islands

Because of its advantageous position within the Caribbean archipelago, Antigua is a great place to begin an island-hopping cruise. Discover nearby treasures like St. Kitts, St. Lucia, or Barbados, and design a personalized trip across the varied cultures and environments of the Caribbean.

Extended Stay Options

Several cruise lines provide homeporting or extended stays for passengers who would like to spend more time on Antigua's coastlines. This makes for a more immersive experience as it enables you to enjoy the island's nightlife and culture after the sun sets in addition to seeing it during the day.

Special Events and Themed Cruises
Throughout the year, Antigua welcomes a range of themed cruises that will amp up the thrill of your nautical experience. These themed cruises cater to a variety of interests, guaranteeing a unique and unforgettable experience. They include gourmet cruises emphasizing local delicacies and music festivals at sea.

Recommendations and Booking Tips
It's best to book your Antigua cruise well in advance, especially during the busiest times of the year. Examine the cruise schedules and make a note of the Antigua shore excursions that are offered. Remember to check the procedures for obtaining a visa for any additional destinations on the cruise itinerary.

Local Exploration and Shore Excursions
Numerous shore excursions are available as soon as your cruise ship arrives at Antigua. Take a trip through the beautiful jungle, relax on Half Moon Bay's immaculate beaches, or see the historic Nelson's Dockyard. Whether they are interested in history, the outdoors, or leisure, cruise guests may customize their time in Antigua to suit their needs.

The charm of Antigua is not limited to its coastline; it also encompasses the waves' rhythmic dance and the marine exploration that reveals the Caribbean's natural splendor. A cruise to Antigua, whether on a massive liner or a small sailboat, promises an amazing voyage where every port of call is a step into a tropical paradise.

Local Transportation

The idea of discovery beckons as soon as you set foot on Antigua's sun-kissed shoreline, and traversing the island's colorful landscapes becomes an essential part of the trip. There are several ways to get about Antigua, from windy drives along coastal roads to strolls through ancient places, so you can make the most of your time here in the Caribbean.

Taxis
On the island, taxis are a common and practical form of transportation. Taxis offer a convenient and pleasant means of transportation whether you're getting off the plane, getting off a cruise, or seeing Antigua. Since taxis don't usually use meters, it's best to negotiate a fee with the driver before you go.

Car Rentals

It's easy to rent a car if you want the flexibility to explore at your speed. You may explore ancient landmarks, wander through quaint towns, and delve into isolated coves while exploring Antigua's well-maintained road network. Remember that you must drive on the left side of the road and that you might need an international driver's license.

Public Transportation

Although not as broad as in other larger places, Antigua's public bus system offers reasonably priced transit. Buses provide a window into local life by connecting popular towns and tourist destinations. For individuals who choose this cost-effective alternative, flexibility is essential as the timetable could be less predictable than with other options.

Cycling

Embrace exploring at a leisurely pace by hiring a bicycle. Riding a bicycle is a pleasant and environmentally beneficial way to see Antigua, thanks to the island's picturesque coastline roads and relatively level terrain. Bicycles for every skill level are available for hire from several stores, and exploring at your own pace fosters a closer relationship with the surroundings.

Water Taxis and Boat Rides

In addition to providing land transit, Antigua has a beautiful coastline and several harbors. For those who are staying near the waterfront or want to take a scenic boat ride across the pristine Caribbean waters, several spots on the island may be easily reached by water taxis and boat transfers.

Tours Guides
Take part in guided excursions that will take you on a physical journey while telling you the fascinating tales of Antigua's past and present. Local tour guides offer insightful commentary, bringing you to hidden jewels and sharing their enthusiasm for the island on both private and scheduled group trips.

Trails Throughout Time
Due to its small size and fascinating history, Antigua is a great place to explore on foot. Explore St. John's cobblestone streets, wander through verdant surroundings, or take a stroll around historic locations like Nelson's Dockyard. Strolling about the island reveals its allure at a relaxed pace, making for chance finds as you go.

Every traveler's tastes are catered to by Antigua's local transportation alternatives, making the trip just as enjoyable as the destination. Depending on your preference—the ease of cabs, the flexibility of a rental vehicle, or the environmentally friendly appeal of bicycles—each means of transportation highlights a distinct aspect of this paradisiacal Caribbean island, beckoning you to see Antigua at your speed.

CHAPTER THREE

Antigua's Hotel Options

Selecting the ideal lodging in Antigua is about more than simply choosing a place to sleep; it's about fully embracing the allure of the island and turning each day of your visit into a chapter of a tropical story. Antigua's housing options are diverse and may accommodate the tastes of every tourist, ranging from opulent resorts situated along immaculate beaches to small, boutique hotels that embody the essence of the island.

Opulent Resorts
Antigua is home to several top-notch resorts that are redefining what it means to be pampered. From the grandiose Sandals Grande Antigua Resort & Spa to the more subtle elegance of Carlisle Bay, these resorts provide a variety of services in addition to luxurious lodging, such as fine dining, spa treatments, and water sports.

Boutique Hotels
Antigua's boutique hotels provide a distinctive fusion of comfort and regional flavor for those looking for a more private and customized stay. With its waterfront location and old architecture, the Admiral's Inn, which is tucked away in the historic Nelson's Dockyard, perfectly

captures this charm. A home away from home atmosphere is created by the personalized services that boutique hotels frequently provide.

Getaways

There are several places along Antigua's coast where you may stay and wake up to the sound of the Caribbean Sea. Stay at upscale resorts by the sea, such as Jumby Bay Island, where isolated beaches and private villas provide a luxurious escape. Beach resorts offer easy access to the island's well-known shorelines in addition to breathtaking vistas.

Classic Style

Select a hotel that pays homage to Antigua's colonial past to fully immerse yourself in its heritage. In Nelson's Dockyard, the Copper and Lumber Store Hotel combines contemporary luxury with historic charm. Remaining in such lodgings is a singular chance to experience a bygone era while relishing modern conveniences.

Economical Choices

Visitors on a tight budget don't have to forgo comfort when visiting Antigua. Cozy lodging is available at several guesthouses and inexpensive hotels, all without compromising the authentic island experience. For instance, the Catamaran Hotel offers great sea views without sacrificing budget.

Inclusive Happiness

Antigua's all-inclusive hotels provide worry-free vacationing for individuals who value convenience. For example, all-inclusive packages at Pineapple Beach Club and Galley Bay Resort & Spa include meals, beverages, and even water sports, freeing up visitors to concentrate only on leisure and enjoyment.

Eco-Friendly Retreats

Antigua's growing number of eco-friendly hotels is a testament to its dedication to sustainability. Tucked up on a mountainside, the Sugar Ridge Hotel promotes environmental responsibility in addition to providing amazing views. These lodging options provide environmentally concerned tourists looking for a peaceful trip in the outdoors.

Reservation Advice

Whatever kind of lodging you choose, it's best to make reservations in advance, especially during popular times. Think about how the location relates to the things you have planned, like seeing historical landmarks, relaxing on the beach, or taking advantage of St. John's exciting nightlife.

Every hotel in Antigua tells a different tale in the tapestry of housing choices, allowing visitors to customize their stay to their liking. The hotels on the island provide more than just a place to sleep—from opulent resorts that indulge your senses to storied inns that take you back in time. They are also the key to discovering the depths of this jewel in the Caribbean.

Antigua's Resorts Options

With its azure seas and sun-kissed beaches, Antigua invites visitors to lose themselves in an extravagant and unwinding world. The island's resorts serve the discriminating tourist looking for more than simply lodging—from opulent all-inclusive getaways to quiet boutique havens. This is a guide to the opulent resorts that turn a trip to Antigua into an experience of a lifetime.

Inclusive Luxurious Experience
Antigua's all-inclusive resorts provide a seamless blend of luxury and convenience for visitors seeking a worry-free getaway. This is best demonstrated by Sandals Grande Antigua Resort & Spa, which is tucked away on the well-known Dickenson Bay and offers a variety of activities, fine dining options, and premium spirits—all of which are included in the package. These resorts provide a refuge where excess is unrestricted.

Premium Island Getaways

The upscale private island resorts in Antigua emphasize privacy and elegance. Only reachable by boat, Jumby Bay Island is a peaceful sanctuary featuring private homes, immaculate beaches, and attentive service. These retreats offer a feeling of seclusion, transforming each second into a uniquely customized experience in a secluded Caribbean paradise.

Beachfront

There are resorts all along Antigua's coastline where you may wake up to the sound of soft waves. Situated on a quiet cove with a natural rainforest backdrop, Carlisle Cove embodies the seaside pleasure that many of the island's resorts have to offer. These resorts immerse visitors in the captivating splendor of the Caribbean Sea, offering everything from private balconies to direct beach access.

Elegant Boutique Style

Antigua's boutique resorts provide a resplendent retreat for anyone looking for a more personal and distinctive experience. Nestled in a picturesque naval environment, The Inn at English Harbour seamlessly blends contemporary elegance with colonial charm. These more intimate resorts provide individualized attention, distinctive decor, and deep cultural immersion.

Healthy Sanctuary Spaces

Antigua's resorts provide comprehensive well-being in addition to enjoyment. With a focus on peace and well-being, Nonsuch Bay Resort provides spa treatments and yoga retreats. Amidst the natural splendor of the Caribbean, these healing sanctuaries provide a balanced blend of relaxation and regeneration.

Safe Havens for Families

Families are welcome in Antigua, where there are resorts for every member. Situated on thirty acres of shoreline, the Verandah Resort & Spa offers a variety of activities fit for guests of all ages in addition to luxurious rooms. Not only do these luxurious getaways cater to families, but they also offer an unforgettable experience for all ages.

Eco-Friendly Getaways

Resorts in Antigua are adopting eco-friendly procedures as sustainability becomes more and more important. The Galley Bay Resort & Spa, which is regarded as Antigua's first green resort, blends elegance and a dedication to environmental care. Resorts that embrace environmental consciousness let their visitors enjoy luxury without feeling guilty.

Booking Points to Remember

When choosing a resort in Antigua, take into account how close it is to the things you want to do, including taking in the exciting nightlife, swimming in the pool, or touring historical landmarks. It is advisable to make reservations in advance, particularly during busy times of the year, to guarantee your desired lodging.

The resorts in Antigua are more than simply places to stay; they serve as entryways to a world of exclusivity, elegance, and Caribbean charm. Every resort has its unique character and promises to provide a haven where the beauty of the island and the art of pleasure are celebrated at every turn.

Vacation Rentals for Tailored Getaways

Vacation rentals provide an alluring alternative to typical lodging for those looking for a more private and customized stay on Antigua's sun-drenched coastlines. Antigua's vacation rentals provide a special chance to enjoy the island's beauty in the comfort of a home away from home, with options ranging from beautiful villas situated on hillsides to beachfront cottages with the sound of the Caribbean lapping at your doorway.

Panoramic View Villa Retreats

Elegant homes with breathtaking views of the Caribbean Sea dot Antigua's slopes. Imagine seeing sailboats drifting over the horizon as you wake up. Not only do rentals such as the Falmouth View Villa offer privacy, but they also give you the ability to enjoy expansive views from your own patio or infinity pool.

Private Cottages

Antigua's beachfront vacation rentals comprehend the draw of being directly on the beach. Guests may walk straight onto the sandy shoreline from private cottages like the Yepton Estate Cottages, forging a close bond with the Caribbean. These exclusive hideaways give a feeling of seclusion and tranquility, redefining the beach holiday.

Historic Homes

Vacation rentals in Antigua are a reflection of the island's colonial past. Antigua's naval past is revealed through historic residences like The Carriage House, which is close to Nelson's Dockyard and has an air of classic beauty. These apartments provide modern luxuries while immersing tourists in the heritage of the island.

Rainforest Retreats

Antigua offers vacation accommodations that go right into the lush jungle for those looking for a more intimate experience with the natural world. Cozy hideaways such as the Fig Tree House offer privacy along with the opportunity to wake up to the sounds of chirping tropical birds. These rentals provide a tasteful fusion of ease and unspoiled beauty.

Beachfront Flats

Chic coastal apartments are available for holiday rentals in Antigua's major hubs, especially St. John's. Antigua Village Beach Club and similar establishments offer a chic and practical starting point for discovering the island's capital. These rentals blend the glamor of the Caribbean Sea with urban elegance.

Family-Friendly Vacation Rental Properties

Large, kid-friendly apartments are one way that vacation rentals appeal to families. For example, The Pineapple House offers a warm and inviting atmosphere suitable for people of all ages. These vacation rental houses guarantee that each family member has an unforgettable Antiguan getaway.

Recommendations and Booking Tips

When making your Antigua vacation rental reservation, take into account the location of the activities you have scheduled and the amount of privacy you want. Fully functional kitchens, private pools, and outside areas are common features of vacation rentals, offering a cozy and self-sufficient getaway.

Vacation homes in Antigua are invites to weave your own story into the colorful fabric of the island, not just a place to stay. Every rental property offers a unique getaway where the rhythms of Antigua become a part of your own, whether it's a historic house with tales to tell, a beachside cottage where the waves become your lullaby or a quiet villa perched on a hill.

Popular Areas to Stay

As you go out to discover Antigua's ideal refuge, the island reveals a varied range of areas and districts, every possessing a distinct allure. Popular places to stay in Antigua include lively beach getaways and historic locations with a rich colonial past, catering to the tastes of many types of travelers. This book will assist you in discovering the unique features of this Caribbean treasure.

The Vibrant Capital
St. John's, the thriving city of Antigua, is a buzzing center full of historic attractions, colorful marketplaces, and a lively vibe. Staying in St. John's puts you close to the island's cultural center, where colonial architecture lines the streets and vibrant markets provide a real

experience of Antiguan life. Accommodations vary from elegant apartments by the shore to contemporary hotels.

English Harbour

English Harbour, which is tucked away on the southern coast, is a charming and historically rich marine sanctuary. This region, which is home to the well-known Nelson's Dockyard, has retained naval architecture and radiates colonial elegance. You may experience the rich maritime history of English Harbour while lodging in luxurious hotels. Popular communities in this area are Freeman's Bay and the scenic Falmouth.

Dickenson Bay

Dickenson Bay is the place to go if your dream vacation includes waking up to the tranquil sound of waves and wide-open vistas of the beach. This region provides a variety of beachfront resorts and vacation homes and is well-known for its immaculate white sands and turquoise seas. Water activities and strolls after dusk are easily accessible, making Dickenson Bay a popular destination for beach lovers.

Jolly Harbour

Jolly Harbour is a marina getaway on the western coast where enjoying life by the sea is the main attraction. This neighborhood is bisected by a man-made canal that is dotted with brightly colored homes and boats. Jolly

Harbour accommodations offer easy access to a restaurant, a golf facility, and a bustling social scene. This region is very well-liked by those who want to experience Antigua from the water.

Runaway Bay
Hiding away on the northwest coast, Runaway Bay provides a quiet haven for individuals in search of peace. This region is renowned for its secluded resorts, verdant landscapes, and peaceful beaches. Runaway Bay lodgings give visitors a route out of the busy tourist areas so they may relax in quiet privacy.

Nonsuch Bay
Nonsuch Bay, which lies on the east coast, is a sailing haven renowned for its pristine surroundings and tranquil seas. For those wishing to cruise the Caribbean by boat, the region is a sanctuary with its opulent resorts and vacation homes. For those looking for a peaceful getaway with access to water sports, Nonsuch Bay is the perfect destination.

Recommendations and Booking Tips
Think about your favorite things to do in Antigua, such as taking in the local culture, going on water sports, or touring historical places, while deciding where to stay. It's best to make reservations in advance, especially

during busy times of the year, to guarantee a place at the location of your choice.

Popular places to stay in Antigua are more than simply sites; they serve as entry points to various aspects of the island's charm. Every piece of this Caribbean paradise encourages you to weave your own story into the vivid tapestry, whether you choose the beachside serenity of Dickenson Bay, the nautical elegance of English Harbour, or the historical depth of St. John's.

CHAPTER FOUR

A Tour through Historical Sites

Beyond being a Caribbean paradise with sun-kissed beaches and crystal-clear waters, Antigua is also a storehouse of rich history, as seen by its colonial architecture and historical sites. The island provides a fascinating collection of historical sites that tell tales of tenacity, maritime prowess, and cultural change for those who have a flair for researching the past. This is a how-to guide for exploring Antigua's eternal echoes.

Nelson's Dockyard

Nelson's Dockyard, the gem in Antigua's naval tradition, is located in the center of English Harbour. The Dockyard, which bears Admiral Horatio Nelson's name, was a vital British naval station in the eighteenth century. It is now recognized as a UNESCO World Heritage Site, conserving the spirit of nautical history in addition to historic structures. Explore the renovated naval structures, such as the Admiral's Inn, the Copper and Lumber Store, and the Dockyard Museum, where displays and relics eloquently narrate the history of the island's naval forces.

Shirley Heights

Shirley Heights is a historical monument with panoramic views of Antigua's southern coast. It is perched atop the verdant hills overlooking English Harbour. Dating back to the 18th century, the reconstructed military lookout and gun battery offer a fascinating peek into the island's defensive history. Come on Sunday nights for the legendary Shirley Heights Lookout Party, where the flamboyant colors of a Caribbean sunset meld with live music to create a unique environment.

Betty's Hope
Discover the agricultural past of Antigua at Betty's Hope, a former 17th-century sugar plantation. The island's once-burgeoning sugar industry is preserved in the twin windmills and the ruins of the sugar processing plants. Explore the educational exhibit and stroll around the fields to get a better understanding of the complicated legacy of slavery and the tenacity of the people who built Antigua's past.

St. John's Cathedral
St. John's Cathedral shines brightly as a symbol of ecclesiastical grace in the center of the capital. Constructed during the 1800s, the cathedral features a remarkable neo-baroque design and is home to the burial of Sir Thomas Warner, the initial governor of the island. In the middle of St. John's bustle, the inside is decorated with exquisite stained glass windows and detailed

wooden carvings, offering a tranquil place for introspection.

Devil's Bridge

Antigua's historical tapestry includes natural treasures like Devil's Bridge in addition to man-made buildings. The unrelenting Atlantic Ocean forces have shaped this natural limestone arch, which is significant both historically and culturally. A local tradition states that in an attempt to escape tyranny, slaves once jumped over the bridge into the turbulent waters below. Devil's Bridge serves as a moving reminder of both the island's turbulent past and the tenacity of its inhabitants today.

Fort James

Fort James is positioned as a watchtower overlooking St. John's Harbour along the northwest shore. Constructed by the British during the 18th century, the fort was ideally situated to fend off any incursions. Discover the island's military past by exploring the well-preserved walls, cannons, and dungeons while taking in breathtaking views of the coastline.

Recommendations and Booking Tips

Take into account the positions of these places about your selected lodging when organizing your historical excursion of Antigua. For certain places, there are guided excursions that offer insightful perspectives into the history of the island.

The historical landmarks of Antigua narrate a story that never stops, allowing visitors to walk in the shoes of people who influenced the fate of the island. Every visit to one of these locations—from the agricultural heritage of Betty's Hope to the nautical majesty of Nelson's Dockyard—reveals a new aspect of Antigua's fascinating past, making every step an adventure through time.

The Natural Wonders of Antigua

There is a world of natural delights waiting to be discovered beyond the postcard-perfect beaches and crystal-clear waters that define Antigua. Encircled by the Caribbean Sea, the island presents a plethora of vistas, ranging from verdant jungles to captivating coral reefs. This is a guide to Antigua's natural wonders, beckoning you to explore the stunning landscape of the island.

Nature's Sculpture at Devil's Bridge
Devil's Bridge, sculpted by the Atlantic Ocean's unrelenting might, is evidence of nature's artistic ability. Situated on the northeastern shore, this naturally occurring limestone arch offers a stunning picture with

crashing waves producing a symphony of noises. In addition to its geological significance, Devil's Bridge has a mythological quality that enhances its already alluring appearance. It is deeply ingrained in local tradition.

Stingray City

Explore Stingray City below the surface to witness an enthralling underwater ballet. This sandbar, off the coast of Antigua, is home to a group of placid southern stingrays. Take a unique look at the colorful marine life of the Caribbean by swimming or snorkeling with these elegant animals in their natural environment.

Shirley Heights

Shirley Heights is well known for its historical significance, but it's also a mountaintop paradise with stunning views of Antigua's southern shore. The expansive vistas that include English Harbour, Falmouth Harbour, and the far-off hills make this an excellent spot to capture the essence of the island's natural beauty. Come on Sunday nights for the Shirley Heights Lookout Party, when the setting sun creates a rainbow-colored panorama.

Fig Tree Drive

Along Fig Tree Drive, discover the center of Antigua's verdant jungle. This picturesque path meanders through lush vegetation, providing views of rare plants, lofty trees, and obscure waterfalls. Take a stroll or take a drive through the rainforest to experience the tranquil sounds of the environment and the vivid colors of the tropical vegetation.

Half Moon Bay

Hiding away on the east coast, Half Moon Bay embodies the unspoiled privacy that so many of Antigua's beaches provide. This crescent-shaped bay beckons peace and leisure with its turquoise seas and fine white dunes. Take a stroll down the beachfront or enjoy the warmth of the sun while taking in Half Moon Bay's unspoiled beauty.

Hercules' Pillars

The Pillars of Hercules are a perfect example of Antigua's untamed beauty. The sea's turquoise hue is dramatically contrasted with these naturally occurring limestone rocks, sculpted by centuries of erosion. The Pillars of Hercules, which are situated on the eastern tip of the island, provide a remote and untamed coastline scenery that is perfect for nature lovers and photographers.

Frigate Bird Sanctuary on Barbuda

Abundant Birdlife: For those who enjoy the outdoors, Barbuda's Frigate Bird Sanctuary is a must-see, even though it's only a short boat journey from Antigua. Nestled in Codrington Lagoon on the island, the sanctuary is home to a large colony of frigate birds. During mating season, observe the sight of these magnificent birds in their native habitat, showcasing their characteristic crimson neck pouches.

Recommendations and Booking Tips
While it is possible to independently discover many of Antigua's natural treasures, guided excursions are offered for those who want more in-depth knowledge and insider knowledge. When organizing your environmental adventure, take into account seasonal fluctuations, such as the best times of year to go snorkeling or the times when birds nest.

The natural beauties of Antigua are invites to fully experience the unadulterated beauty of the Caribbean, not only breathtaking scenery. Each natural wonder adds a layer to the symphony of feelings that characterizes Antigua's attraction, whether you're standing on the towering arch of Devil's Bridge, exploring the rainforest along Fig Tree Drive, or swimming with stingrays in the blue seas.

Antigua's Cultural Events

Antigua's colorful culture emerges as the sun sets, creating a rhythmic tapestry that reflects the history, customs, and exuberance of the island. Travelers are welcome to immerse themselves in Antigua's cultural activities, which range from vibrant festivals honoring local artists to lively music that fills the streets. This is an itinerary of Antigua's exciting events to make sure you don't miss the sounds and rhythms that characterize the island's vibrant spirit.

Antigua Carnival

The Antigua Carnival is the highlight of the island's cultural calendar, a kaleidoscope of hues, melodies, and contagious enthusiasm. Every year, in late July or early August, vivid parades, spectacular costumes, and throbbing rhythms fill the streets of St. John's. Steelpan orchestras offer a Caribbean touch, while the soundtrack is composed of calypso and soca music. Don't miss the thrilling J'ouvert morning, when the carnival celebrations begin as revelers dance around the streets coated in powder and paint.

Independence Day Celebrations on Wadadli Day

Wadadli Day, on November 1st, commemorates the independence of Antigua and Barbuda and is a cultural event that highlights the country's history. Vibrant parades, traditional dance performances, and the presentation of Antiguan food are all part of the festivities. At this lively event, join the people in celebrating their rich history and cultural identity.

Cultural Explosion

An annual celebration of the richness of Antiguan and Caribbean art, the Cultural Explosion takes place in April. The festival showcases the abilities of local and regional artists with an enthralling blend of visual arts, theater, dance, and music. With events ranging from modern art exhibits to traditional steel pan shows, Cultural Explosion offers a thorough look into the island's creative life.

Antigua and Barbuda International Literary Festival

The Antigua and Barbuda International Literary Festival, which takes place every November, is a must-see for fans of literature. Poets, writers, and readers from all over the world come together for provocative conversations, book signings, and cross-cultural interactions. Amidst the picturesque scenery of Antigua, the event fosters an appreciation for literature and stimulating intellectual discourse.

Independence Calypso Competition

The Independence Calypso Competition is a display of musical prowess and reflects the unique role calypso music has in Antigua's cultural fabric. Talented calypsonians fight for the coveted title in this tournament, which is held as part of the nation's Independence Day celebrations. The lyrics provide a distinct viewpoint on the state of events on the island by frequently touching on social concerns, politics, and cultural views.

John's Day

June 24th is St. John's Day, a religious and cultural celebration honoring the capital city's patron saint. A religious parade through the streets opens the day, which is then followed by music, dance, and traditional Antiguan cuisine. St. John's Day offers a distinctive fusion of religious celebration and cultural revelry, attracting both residents and tourists to join in the fun.

Nagico Super50 Cricket Tournament

The Nagico Super50 Cricket Tournament, although not a customary cultural occasion, is evidence of Antigua's love of sports, particularly cricket. This regional cricket competition, which fosters a sense of friendship and sports spirit, draws teams throughout the Caribbean and is held at the Sir Vivian Richards Stadium. Fans of cricket may watch exciting matches in the welcoming atmosphere of Antigua.

Recommendations and Booking Tips

If you're basing your trip around a particular cultural event, be sure to check the itinerary and book your lodging in advance. Since many cultural events have a set date associated with them, timing your visit to coincide with these celebrations can guarantee a more thorough experience.

Cultural events in Antigua are more than just planned activities; they are manifestations of the spirit of the island, with every rhythm and tune speaking to the hearts of its residents. Every cultural event, whether it's dancing in the streets during Carnival or participating in literary discussions during the Literary Festival, encourages you to join the lively pace that characterizes Antigua's cultural fabric.

CHAPTER FIVE

An Overview of the Island's Stunning Beaches

An exquisite chain of immaculate beaches, each with its distinct personality and appeal, encircles Antigua, a treasure of the Caribbean. Antigua's beaches welcome visitors to relax in paradisiacal beauty, offering everything from quiet coves surrounded by beautiful scenery to long expanses of powdered white sand meeting the blue embrace of the Caribbean Sea. This is a guide to the shoreline symphony of the island to help you find the gems around the coast that suit your perfect beach getaway.

Dickenson Bay
Located on the northwest coast of the island, Dickenson Bay embodies the epitome of sun-kissed beauty. This long stretch of white sand beach is bordered by blue seas and palm trees that sway softly. Dickenson Bay is well-known for having calm seas, making it the perfect place for swimming, snorkeling, and other water activities. Beach bars and eateries along the shore, provide the ideal combination of laid-back vibes and lively energy.

Half Moon Bay

Half Moon Bay, hidden away on Antigua's eastern coast, is the pinnacle of remote beauty. Reachable along a meandering shoreline path, this crescent-shaped cove features powdery pink beaches and is surrounded by craggy rocks. Half Moon Bay's isolation adds to its charm, offering a peaceful haven for those longing for tranquility. Savor the unspoiled beauty of this undiscovered gem by taking a stroll down the coast or lounging in the sun.

Darkwood Beach

Situated on the southwest side of the island, Darkwood Beach has a tranquil Caribbean atmosphere. This charming beach has golden sands that smoothly blend into the glistening waves. It is surrounded by lush vegetation. Darkwood Beach is a great place to swim and snorkel because of the calm surf and the surrounding foliage offers a natural haven. In addition, coastal eateries with regional specialties are available to beachgoers.

Galley Bay

Galley Bay, tucked away on the western coast, provides a peaceful sanctuary for those looking for a quiet getaway. This beach is well-known for its gentle beaches and tranquil atmosphere. It is bordered by palm palms and blue waves. It's a great place to swim and paddleboard because of the calm waters. It is the perfect place for day visitors as well as resort guests, with a picturesque backdrop provided by the nearby Galley Bay Resort & Spa.

Pigeon Point Beach
The beach at Pigeon Point, which is close to English Harbour, combines historical charm with scenic splendor. The beach is surrounded by colonial-era buildings because it is located next to the famous Nelson's Dockyard. Before resting on Pigeon Point Beach's charming sands, tourists may explore the neighboring historical monuments. The beach's tranquil waters make it ideal for swimming and snorkeling.

Jolly Beach
Jolly Beach on the southwest coast is a bustling beach with wide sands that evoke energetic vibes. This well-liked beach is well-known for its lively atmosphere, water sports, and seaside bars. Because Jolly Beach is a center of activity, it's a great option for anyone looking for a vibrant beach experience. Both leisure and recreation are catered to by the vibrant surroundings and crystal-clear seas.

Valley Church Beach
Valley Church Beach, which is on the western shore, provides a view of the Caribbean's blue seas and fine white beaches. The beach has calm waters and

breathtaking views of the far-off islands, making it a great place to swim and snorkel. The beach is lined with vibrant umbrellas and beach bars, making it the perfect place for a day of indulgence by the sea.

Recommendations and Booking Tips
When organizing your Antigua beach getaway, take into account how close your preferred lodging is to the beach. Although many beaches are open to the public, some could include features exclusive to those staying at resorts. It is advised to make reservations in advance, particularly during busy times of the year, to guarantee beachfront lodging.

The beaches of Antigua are more than simply locations to enjoy the sunshine; they are canvases adorned with Caribbean hues, beckoning you to immerse yourself in the calm waves, feel the smooth sand beneath your feet, and let the sea's harmonious sounds captivate your senses. There is a beach for every type of paradise seeker along Antigua's coastline, whether you're looking for bustling coastal vibes or quiet seclusion.

Antigua's Water Sports

Encircled by the soft embrace of the Caribbean Sea, Antigua invites thrill-seekers to its watery playground, where a variety of exhilarating water sports may be enjoyed in the turquoise seas. Water lovers will find an exciting range of activities on the island, from the peaceful discovery of snorkeling to the explosive rush of windsurfing. This guide to Antigua's water sports spectacular will make sure you embark on an aquatic journey you won't soon forget.

Windsurfing

Antigua is a windsurfing haven because of its consistent trade winds and warm seas. Windsurfers of all skill levels may take advantage of the Caribbean breeze at places like Dickenson Bay and Jabberwock Beach. You may rent equipment and receive instruction from windsurfing schools along the coast, enabling you to ride the waves with assurance and proficiency.

Kitesurfing

For those looking for an exhilarating experience, kitesurfing is the main attraction. Jabberwock Beach is a popular destination for kitesurfers due to its steady breezes. Feel the incredible rush of this exciting water activity as you glide over the waves, driven by the wind. All skill levels are catered for at kitesurfing courses, guaranteeing a thrilling and risk-free experience.

Diving Underwater for Submerged Peace

Snorkeling offers a doorway to peaceful submersion, and Antigua's undersea world is a treasure trove just waiting to be discovered. Bright marine life abounds on coral reefs, and secluded coves provide vistas of colorful fish and intriguing seascapes. Cades Reef and Stingray City are well-liked snorkeling locations that offer a vibrant underwater experience in the Caribbean.

Deep Sea Exploration using Scuba Diving

Discover a world of undersea marvels by going on scuba diving trips into the Caribbean Sea's depths. Divers of all skill levels may enjoy Antigua's diving destinations, which include the Pillars of Hercules and the Andes Wreck. Deep-sea exploration on the island is accessible to both novice and expert divers thanks to the certification courses offered by dive schools.

Canoeing

Experience the peace of exploring the coastline by going kayaking around Antigua's shorelines. Witness the island's splendor drenched in the golden colors of the evening by going on kayaking trips at sunset, exploring secret coves, or paddling through mangroves. With the option of guided excursions or kayak rentals, you may explore the waterways at your speed.

Balance and Happiness with Stand-Up Paddleboarding (SUP)

Explore the ideal harmony between calmness and exhilaration through stand-up paddling. SUP aficionados will find the placid waters at Ffryes Beach and Jolly Harbour to be ideal. Antigua's SUP scene offers beautiful moments on the water, regardless of skill level. Perfect for beginners learning to balance or seasoned paddlers looking for a tranquil coastal cruise.

Jet Skiing

Jet skiing around Antigua's coasts is an exhilarating experience for individuals who are itching for a rush of speed and thrills. Feel the rush of the water beneath you and the wind in your hair as you zip across the waves of the Caribbean. Many beaches offer jet ski trips with guides and rental options.

Deep-Sea Fishing

Deep-sea fishing prospects in Antigua appeal to passionate fishermen looking for a marine experience. Take advantage of fishing excursions to explore the vast oceans in search of marlin, tuna, and other impressive captures. Every deep-sea fishing trip offers the opportunity to reel in thrills and rewards thanks to the island's abundant marine life.

Recommendations and Booking Tips

In Antigua, hotels, resorts, or specialist water sports facilities may arrange for a variety of water sports activities. When making reservations for water sports activities, take into account your interests, ability level, and the weather. It is advised to make reservations in advance, particularly during the busiest travel seasons.

The aquatic attractions on Antigua are more than just things to do; they open doors to the spirit of the island, unveiling a world of undersea wonders and exhilarating pleasures. Whether you're kayaking along tranquil coasts, windsurfing across the Caribbean air, or snorkeling amid colorful coral gardens, all of these water sports guarantee an immersion into Antigua's dynamic and enchanted aquatic playground.

Antigua Hiking Experiences

Antigua's natural beauty is shown in a new way when you venture past the sun-kissed beaches and crystal-clear seas. These routes run through verdant landscapes, ancient monuments, and breathtaking overlooks. If you're looking to put on your hiking boots and explore the island's varied landscape, Antigua has several paths suitable for different levels of experience. This guide to trail tales in Antigua invites you to go on trekking trips you won't soon forget.

Fig Tree Drive

Hiking along Fig Tree Drive, a picturesque path through Antigua's jungle, will transport you to a world of tropical grandeur. The route showcases the island's abundant flora and animals as it passes through beautiful surroundings. Discover towering trees, colorful wildlife, and the calming sounds of nature as you explore this fantasy jungle. For hikers of all skill levels, Fig Tree Drive offers an ideal introduction to Antigua's natural splendor.

Monk's Hill Trail

Monk's Hill Trail offers a trip through time and elevation for both history buffs and serious hikers. The walk begins close to English Harbour and climbs to Monk's Hill, where the remains of Fort George serve as silent reminders of Antigua's nautical past. When one reaches the historically significant heights, the expansive vistas from the peak take in English Harbor, Falmouth Harbor, and the far horizon.

Shirley Heights

Shirley Heights is well known for its historical significance, but there is also a physical aspect to the experience thanks to the hiking track that leads to the peak. The walk climbs through dense foliage from Galleon Beach to the famous viewpoint. This climb is perfect for individuals who want a mix of history and natural beauty since it rewards effort with stunning views of English Harbour.

Signal Hill

Signal Hill provides coastal attractiveness with hikes and spectacular seascapes, just near Nelson's Dockyard entrance. The route meanders along the craggy shore, offering views of the Pillars of Hercules and the blue waters of the Caribbean. For individuals who want to experience seaside sights without embarking on an extensive excursion, this relatively short hike is a great option.

Boggy Peak

Boggy Peak, also called Mount Obama, is the highest peak on the island and challenges climbers to reach the highest point in Antigua. The Boggy Peak trek winds across the island's central highlands and provides a strenuous but worthwhile climb. A sensation of wonder and achievement is created in hikers upon reaching the peak, where they are rewarded with expansive views of Antigua and its nearby islands.

Carpenter Rock Trail

Carpenter Rock Trail is a biodiversity sanctuary for nature lovers and birdwatchers. This path, which is close to the Shekerley Mountains, passes through limestone scrublands and dry woods, among other types of habitats. Birdwatchers can see both migratory and native species, making this a special trip that blends environmental study with breathtaking vistas.

Ridge to Fort Barrington
A diverse hiking experience is provided by the Ridge to Fort Barrington walk, which combines historical history with coastal exploration. The route travels to the well-preserved Fort Barrington by following the hill that overlooks the Caribbean Sea, starting from Deep Bay. A wonderful fusion of history and environment may be experienced by hikers as they explore the fort's remains and take in expansive views of the coastline.

Recommendations and Booking Tips
Before starting a hiking trip in Antigua, think about the trail's length, difficulty, and degree of fitness. A navigation guide may be necessary for certain paths, particularly those that have historical sites. Make sure you have enough water with you, dress in proper shoes, and check the weather before you go.

Hiking paths in Antigua are more than simply routes; they tell stories about the island's past and present. Hiking through jungles, scaling ancient peaks, or discovering the allure of the shore, every path presents a different angle on Antigua's breathtaking scenery. Put on your hiking boots, go for the trails, and let Antigua's natural treasures lead the way.

CHAPTER SIX

Antigua Local Cuisine Experiences

Antigua's food scene comes to life as the sun sets over the Caribbean, presenting a symphony of tastes that honor the island's rich cultural legacy. Antigua welcomes visitors on a gourmet adventure that represents the diversity of its people and the abundance of its land and sea. This journey includes everything from lively street markets to seaside shacks and fine waterfront restaurants. This is a guide to help you fully enjoy Antigua's diverse culinary scene and capture the spirit of the island's regional cuisine.

Street Food
Start your gastronomic journey by discovering Antigua's thriving street food scene, where regional sellers present the tastes of the island in a relaxed and genuine environment. Come enjoy some fresh fruit, delicious pastries, and traditional Antiguan snacks at St. John's Saturday Morning Market with the locals. Try the popular "fungi and pepper pot," which consists of a hearty pork stew and cornmeal dumplings.

Fridays with Fish at Gourmet Capital
Be ready for a seafood bonanza if you find yourself in the quaint community of English Harbour on a Friday

evening. Fish Fridays turn Gourmet Capital, as it's often called, into a busy street carnival. Locals erect booths with grilled lobster, conch fritters, and an assortment of recently caught fish for offer. Savor the abundance of the ocean under the stars while taking in the vibrant atmosphere and live music.

Savoring Breakfast in Antigua

Antiguan breakfast staples fill you with delectable fragrances as you wake up. Savor "saltfish and fungi," a flavorful dish consisting of salted codfish combined with cornmeal dumplings, okra, and seasonings from the area, at a nearby restaurant or the restaurant inside your lodging. A generous portion of "bakes," or deep-fried dough, completes this satisfying Antiguan meal to start the day.

Indian Influences on Roti and Doubles

Indian culinary traditions have left their mark on Antigua's cuisine, as evidenced by dishes like roti and doubles. Flatbreads called roti are frequently stuffed with curried meats, veggies, or chickpeas to provide a filling and tasty meal. A popular street food item, doubles are made of two flatbreads with curried chickpeas in between. Visit your neighborhood markets or specialized restaurants to enjoy these delectable Indian-inspired sweets.

Casual Dining by the Water

Antigua's coastal appeal makes it home to a plethora of waterfront eateries where you can savor seafood feasts while taking in the gorgeous scenery. Select from an array of freshly caught seafood, such as snapper, mahi-mahi, and lobster, all of which are skillfully cooked using regional herbs and spices. For the ideal beachside dining experience, pair your meal with cool coconut water or rum punch.

Food Festivals and Culinary Events

You are in luck if your visit coincides with one of Antigua's food festivals or gourmet events. Restaurants that participate in events like Antigua and Barbuda Restaurant Week provide unique menus and specials, showcasing the island's various culinary choices. Another highlight is the Wadadli Food and Rum Festival, which offers live entertainment, rum tastings, and a blend of regional and foreign cuisines.

Nearby Desserts and Bush Tea

Enjoy the herbal customs of Antigua by sampling the bush teas made from a range of therapeutic plants and herbs. Serve your tea with "sugar cake" or "black pineapple tart," two classic Antiguan sweets that will provide a delightful finish to your meal. Stop by markets or bakeries in your area to enjoy these delicious delicacies.

Recommendations and Booking Tips

When discovering Antigua's native cuisine, take advantage of the chance to interact with the people there, seek advice, and be willing to try different dishes. Make reservations at well-known restaurants to guarantee your place, and look for any local events or festivals taking place during your stay.

Antigua's food scene is a kaleidoscope of tastes, fusing elements from its African background, Caribbean origins, and international ties. Every bite and drink of Antigua's culinary legacy tells a narrative, making every meal a memorable aspect of your island trip, whether you're indulging in street food delights, feasting on seafood by the ocean, or exploring the subtleties of regional bush teas.

Antigua's Popular Restaurants and Cafés

In addition to its sun-kissed beaches and lively culture, Antigua has a diverse food scene to suit all tastes. The island's eating businesses guarantee a gourmet trip enhanced by regional tastes and global influences, ranging from sophisticated waterfront restaurants with panoramic views to intimate cafés nestled away in old alleys. This is a list of some of the well-known eateries and cafés in Antigua that invite you to savor a wide range of gastronomic delights.

Sheer Rocks

Elegance and fine dining are personified at Sheer Rocks, which is perched on a rock with a view of Ffryes Bay. This restaurant serves food with a Mediterranean flair that is made using ingredients that are acquired locally. Savor delectable delicacies like ceviche, slow-cooked lamb, and decadent desserts while dining on chic daybeds or at the edge of the cliff. Sheer Rocks offers a multi-sensory experience that includes stunning vistas, flawless service, and more than simply a meal.

Cecilia's High Point Café

Nestled on a hillside near Dutchman's Bay, Cecilia's High Point Café offers a little haven with expansive vistas. The menu has a range of seafood, grilled meats, and vegetarian selections, combining Caribbean and international influences. Friendly service and a relaxed vibe make it a favorite destination for residents and tourists looking for delicious food and charming hilltop views.

Le Bistro

Le Bistro, which is situated in the picturesque English Harbour, adds a bit of French flare to Antigua's culinary scene. The restaurant, which is situated in a lovely courtyard, provides a cozy atmosphere in which to enjoy traditional French fare with a Caribbean touch. Le Bistro embraces the native delicacies of the island while transporting customers to the heart of France with dishes like coq au vin and escargot.

Papa Zouk

A trip to Papa Zouk in St. John's is a must if you want to sample the colorful tastes of the Caribbean and have a rum-centric experience. Seafood dishes served with a Caribbean flair are the restaurant's specialty. It is well-known for its large range of rum and vibrant ambiance. This well-known seafood haven's appeal is enhanced by its rustic charm and communal eating area.

The Admiral's Inn

A gastronomic jewel with a nautical elegance, The Admiral's Inn is located within the historic Nelson's Dockyard. The restaurant, which is housed in a renovated 18th-century structure, serves a fusion of Caribbean and world food. Take in the atmosphere of nautical heritage while dining on the patio with a view of the harbor and food that is expertly and creatively prepared.

Jacqui O's BeachHouse

Situated on the sandy shores of Ffryes Beach, Jacqui O's BeachHouse is the pinnacle of beachside elegance. An elegant oceanfront dining experience is provided by the restaurant, which has stylish décor and white linens. With a focus on fresh seafood, the menu offers an unusual blend of foreign and Caribbean cuisine. At this chic dining spot, savor handmade drinks while taking in the breathtaking sunset views.

Cloggy's Café

Tucked away in a peaceful cove near English Harbour, Cloggy's Café offers a seaside haven for those looking to unwind and indulge in delicious food. The cuisine highlights fresh and locally produced foods while showcasing a blend of Caribbean and international tastes. Enjoy a meal on the patio outside while taking in the tranquil sounds of the sea and a plethora of vegetation.

Artisanal Delights

The Larder is a deli and artisanal café in St. John's that serves sophisticated foodies. A variety of gourmet sandwiches, salads, and freshly baked items are available on the menu. It's a well-liked option for breakfast or a relaxed lunch because of the focus on premium products and a welcoming ambiance.

Hemingway's Caribbean Café

Hemingway's Caribbean Café in St. John's, named for the well-known author who used to visit Antigua, has a literary appeal of its own. The café provides a laid-back atmosphere for informal lunches, brunches, and breakfasts. There are several Caribbean-inspired meals, sandwiches, and cool drinks on the menu. For those who want a taste of the island's simple cuisine, Hemingway offers a relaxed haven.

Recommendations and Booking Tips
It is advisable to make reservations, particularly for well-known eateries and during periods of high visitor traffic. For evening service, certain restaurants could have dress rules, so it's best to check ahead. To truly enjoy Antigua's unique gastronomic choices, try a variety of regional and international cuisines.

Popular eateries like Antigua's restaurants and cafés are more than simply places to dine; they're culinary journeys that highlight the originality and diversity of the island. Each dining experience gives a different sense of Antigua's rich culinary tapestry, whether you're relishing French flair in English Harbour, enjoying a riverfront getaway, or indulging in cliffside luxury. Take a culinary tour, savor the tastes, and make Antigua's dining scene the centerpiece of your Caribbean vacation.

Dietary Considerations

A jewel of the Caribbean, Antigua is well-known for its sun-kissed beaches and lively culture, but it also meets a wide range of dietary requirements. The island's restaurants and eateries aim to offer a warm and inclusive eating experience, regardless of whether you're a food explorer discovering regional delicacies or someone with particular dietary needs. This is a guide to helping you navigate Antigua's food scene while taking dietary restrictions into account so that every taste is satisfied.

Vegan & Vegetarian Treats
The vegetarian and vegan communities of Antigua are well-served by the island's diverse plant-based cuisine, which highlights its abundant fresh food. Many eateries showcase the vivid tastes of locally produced foods with inventive salads, veggie stir-fries, and plant-based curries. Seek for restaurants that specifically accommodate vegan and vegetarian diets, and don't be afraid to ask about specialized menu items.

Options Without Gluten
Antigua's eateries are aware of your dietary requirements if you are gluten-free. Gluten-free options may be found on many menus, and chefs are frequently happy to fulfill special requests. A gluten-free meal may

easily include mainstays like seafood, fresh fruit, and grilled meats. To guarantee a smooth and delightful supper, let the staff know what you eat.

Allergy Awareness

The hospitality sector in Antigua is aware of the significance of allergy awareness. When dining out, let the staff know if you have any dietary restrictions or allergies, and they will assist you navigate the menu and make safe selections. Chefs are trained to handle common allergies like dairy, shellfish, and nuts, so guests with dietary sensitivities may eat with confidence.

Sponsorship and Personalization

The utilization of local, fresh ingredients is celebrated in Antigua's culinary scene. A lot of eateries take great satisfaction in serving food prepared with ingredients from the island's markets and farms. Because of their dedication to using only the freshest ingredients, chefs are frequently open to modifying menu items to meet special dietary requirements. Please feel free to express any dietary needs or limitations, and savor a meal that has been specially prepared for you.

Nutritional Factors in Conventional Cooking

The traditional cuisine of Antigua, which has its roots in the history and cultural influences of the island, may be modified to accommodate different dietary needs. One popular local meal, "fungi and pepper pot," for instance, may be made vegetarian or vegan. The chefs in the area are skilled in incorporating customary tastes into meals that suit a variety of dietary requirements.

From Farm-to-Table Encounters

Discover Antigua's farm-to-table dining options, where restaurants emphasize serving organic, locally sourced food. These locations frequently highlight ethical and ecological activities in addition to offering a cuisine that accommodates a variety of dietary requirements. Savor the dishes that reflect the abundance of the island, understanding that your dinner is a celebration of Antigua's rich agricultural heritage.

Fresh Juices and Smoothie Bars

Due to its abundance of tropical fruits, Antigua is a smoothie and juice lover's paradise. Stop by your neighborhood juice bar or smoothie shop to enjoy cool concoctions prepared with fresh fruit and sometimes veggies. For those who prefer lighter cuisine, these selections offer not only a delightful beverage but also a wholesome and hydrating substitute.

Interaction with Employees

To guarantee a satisfying eating experience, it is essential to communicate effectively with restaurant employees. Tell servers of any dietary requirements, allergies, or preferences without holding back. The majority of places are accommodative and ready to change to suit your requirements. Having a cordial conversation with the personnel will make your gastronomic experience more delightful and customized.

Recommendations and Booking Tips
It's best to let the restaurant know in advance if you have particular dietary requirements while booking reservations, especially. This enables the chef to produce meals and alter them to suit your tastes. You should also look into internet reviews or get in touch with the restaurant personally to find out whether they can accommodate special dietary needs.

Antigua's dedication to culinary innovation and diversity is evident in its diverse culinary scene. The island's restaurants are keen to make sure that every visitor has a tasty and fulfilling eating experience, whether they are tackling allergic concerns, discovering gluten-free alternatives, or relishing plant-based delicacies. Therefore, start on a gastronomic adventure with assurance, knowing that Antigua's culinary compass is poised to satisfy and exalt every palette.

CHAPTER SEVEN

Antigua's Local Markets

Take in the dynamic tapestry of Antigua's local marketplaces and embrace the vibrant pulse of its culture. Antigua's markets offer a sensory experience that represents the island's rich tradition, from crowded stalls decorated with exotic fruits to craftsmen displaying handmade products. These markets are an integral part of your Caribbean experience, offering fresh produce, handcrafted goods, and a taste of true Antiguan delicacies.

Saturday Morning Market at St. John's
An abundance of fresh produce: The Saturday Morning Market is the hub of activity for market exploration in St. John's, the capital of Antigua. Every Saturday, the vibrant market turns the city into a veritable oasis of fresh produce. Gathering to display a variety of fruits, vegetables, herbs, and spices are local farmers and sellers. Immerse yourself in the rainbow of hues and fragrances while conversing with amiable vendors who are happy to give information on Antigua's abundant agricultural output as well as their goods.

St. John's Heritage Quay

St. John's Heritage Quay is a popular duty-free shopping area, but it also has a bustling market. Discover the handcrafted crafts of local artisans at the craft and souvenir kiosks. With everything from colorful textiles and elaborate jewelry to ceramics and wood carvings, Heritage Quay provides a special fusion of shopping and cultural discovery. Discover hidden gems that perfectly capture Antigua's creative spirit by strolling through this ancient district.

Redcliffe Quay Market
Redcliffe Quay Market, tucked away in the center of St. John's, radiates colonial elegance and features the skill of regional craftsmen. The cobblestone streets of the market are dotted with shops and vendors selling a variety of handcrafted items, such as apparel, accessories, and mementos. Take in the historical atmosphere while perusing the unique selection and finding one-of-a-kind items that perfectly embody Antiguan workmanship.

The Potters Village Farmers Market
For a sense of community spirit, visit the Farmers Market at Potters Village. Every Saturday, local farmers, artisans, and food merchants congregate at this market. As you browse the fresh fruit, handcrafted items, and homemade treats, take in the vibrant environment. Talk to the welcoming merchants and discover this

neighborhood-based market. You could even pick up a few traditional recipes.

Swallowfield Courtyard
Go to English Harbour's Swallowfield Courtyard for a sophisticated market experience. A carefully chosen assortment of locally manufactured items, artwork, and handcrafted crafts are on display at this artisanal market. Wander around the colorful bougainvillea-filled courtyard and take in the creations of talented craftspeople. Amid the natural beauty of English Harbour, Swallowfield Courtyard provides a refined shopping experience, with anything from unique jewelry items to artwork inspired by the Caribbean.

Liberta Village Market
To experience true Antiguan delicacies, take a trip to Liberta Village and get away from the hustle and bustle of the city. Fridays are dedicated to the Liberta Village Market, a local event when farmers and artisans showcase their wares. Savor the abundant selection of fresh produce, fruits, and regional delicacies. Talk to the merchants and use their enthusiasm for their goods to further your understanding of Antigua's farming legacy.

Artisanal Food Markets
Antigua has artisanal food markets that showcase the island's culinary expertise in addition to its fresh product

offerings. Visit marketplaces that provide regional specialties, freshly prepared sauces, spices, and classic Antiguan cuisine. Take your taste buds on a gourmet adventure and experience the variety of flavors that characterize Antiguan food. These markets offer a special chance to bring the diverse cuisine of the island to your table.

Recommendations and Booking Tips

It's best to have cash while visiting local markets because some sellers might not take credit or debit cards. Be willing to haggle, particularly in places where it's common. If you want to carry your items in a reusable bag, think about doing so. Additionally, don't be hesitant to ask sellers how best to use their products.

The markets in Antigua are more than simply places to buy; they are lively centers that radiate the spirit of the island and highlight the friendliness of its people as well as the diversity of their customs. Every market visit is an adventure through Antigua's cultural legacy, whether you're perusing the Saturday Morning Market in St. John's, ogling handcrafted products at Redcliffe Quay, or tasting regional cuisine at Liberta Village. Enter the busy stalls, strike up a conversation with the locals, and allow the markets to lead you on a genuine and immersive journey into the heart of the Caribbean.

Handmade Items and Souvenirs

It makes sense that when you take in Antigua's bright culture and sun-kissed scenery, you'll want to bring a little bit of the Caribbean home. Thankfully, the island's artisans and craftsmen have produced a wealth of mementos and handicrafts that perfectly capture Antigua's essence. These keepsakes, which range from traditional crafts to handcrafted jewelry, let you take a little piece of the island's allure with you everywhere you go. This is a guide to the distinctive handicrafts and souvenirs you may find in Antigua.

Batik Creations and Handwoven Textiles
The lively culture of Antigua is reflected in the wide variety of handwoven fabrics and batik masterpieces available at the island's artisan markets. Colorful textiles, clothes, and accessories are created by local artists using age-old methods. Dive into the rainbow of colors and patterns, and pick a handwoven fabric or batik item to bring the vibrant energy of the Caribbean into your wardrobe.

Jewelry Embellished with Native Gemstones
Many semi-precious stones may be found in Antigua, and the region's jewelers expertly craft distinctive

jewelry from these jewels. Discover bracelets, necklaces, and earrings embellished with stones like Antiguan jade, which is a brilliant green, and larimar, which is referred to as the "Caribbean gem," by visiting artisan markets and stores. Every component narrates a tale of the geological marvels of the island.

Antiguan Ceramics & Pottery

Rich clay reserves on the island have led to a thriving Antigua pottery industry. Beautiful ceramics, ranging from ornamental items to useful tableware, are crafted by local artists through the molding of clay. Look for handcrafted mugs, bowls, and vases with elaborate designs that capture the essence of the Caribbean's natural beauty by visiting pottery studios and marketplaces.

Veritable Rum from the Caribbean

Consider bringing home a bottle of Antigua's famous rum to have a taste of the island's liquid riches. Numerous rum mixes, each with its own distinct character and flavor profile, are produced by nearby distilleries. A bottle of Antiguan rum is a great memento and a taste of the island's history, regardless of your preference for the spiced or matured kinds.

Carvings and Straw Baskets

Discover the rich cultural legacy of Antigua by engaging with indigenous crafts such as wood carvings and handwoven straw baskets. Expert craftspeople craft elaborate patterns using regional resources to make useful and adornment pieces. These handicrafts give your collection of souvenirs a genuine touch by frequently including images from Caribbean life.

Art Inspired by the Island
Local artists have been inspired to produce beautiful works of art by the vivid colors and breathtaking sceneries of Antigua. Discover sculptures, prints, and paintings that encapsulate the spirit of the island by perusing galleries and marketplaces. These pieces of art offer a visual tour of Antigua's splendor, ranging from images of everyday life to views of tropical flora and animals.

Regional Flavors and Gastronomic Treasures
Beyond its borders, Antigua has a diverse range of sensations, and taking a bit of the island home is simple with locally made spices and delectable foods. In markets and specialized stores, look for spice mixes, spicy sauces, and traditional Antiguan sweets. You may bring back the flavorful memories of Antigua in your kitchen with these tasty keepsakes.

Aloe Vera Products

The temperature of Antigua is perfect for growing aloe vera, which has calming and restorative qualities. Lotions, creams, and balms prepared locally from aloe vera provide a natural and restorative method of treating oneself. These goods, which are frequently created by regional artists, provide useful and considerate mementos.

Recommendations and Booking Tips:
To assure the authenticity of your purchases, think about supporting local markets and artists while making souvenir and handicraft purchases. At traditional stores, haggling is frowned upon, but at outdoor marketplaces, it could be permitted. In particular, look for any prohibitions on returning handcrafted or agricultural goods to your country of origin.

The handicrafts and souvenirs from Antigua are more than simply physical representations of the energy and ingenuity of the island. Every memento becomes a treasured remembrance of your Caribbean vacation, whether you're wearing jewelry created locally, showcasing handcrafted items about your house, or indulging in local cuisine. So explore the marketplaces, talk to knowledgeable craftspeople, and let Antigua's treasures become a part of your life and house.

Antigua's Duty-Free Shopping Extravaganza

Along with being a Caribbean paradise for leisure, Antigua's sun-kissed beaches and lively culture also make it a refuge for duty-free shoppers. The island has a wide variety of products, from high-end labels to handcrafted items from the area, alluring visitors with the prospect of tax-free shopping. This is your guide to Antigua's duty-free shopping, where the excitement of finding unusual items combines with the draw of bargains.

Retail Heaven at Heritage Quay
Situated in the center of St. John's, Heritage Quay is Antigua's most popular duty-free retail area. Numerous foreign and local businesses, selling anything from high-end jewelry and apparel to gadgets and mementos, can be found in this busy complex. Heritage Quay is enticing not only because of its wide selection of products but also because all purchases are free from import charges and municipal taxes.

Duty-Free Shopping & Historic Charm atRedcliffe Quay
Redcliffe Quay, a short distance from Heritage Quay, offers a historic charm-infused retail experience. There are several galleries and stores in this region, which have colonial buildings and cobblestone lanes. Shoppers may

enjoy duty-free prices while perusing the distinctive items, combining modern savings with a pleasant combination of historic ambiance with every purchase.

Outside the Capital Shopping in St. Mary's Street and Other Locations
Although St. John's is a major shopping destination, explore other areas of the country for more duty-free finds. St. Mary's Street, situated in English Harbour, provides duty-free boutique shopping choices. Discover a variety of products here, including apparel, accessories, and handcrafted items made in the area, all while taking in the picturesque views of English Harbour.

V.C. Bird International Airport Luxury Brands
V.C. Bird International Airport is a shopping paradise for those who can't wait to splurge on duty-free goodies before the flight. Duty-free stores at the airport provide a variety of high-end brands of accessories, watches, and fragrances. Travelers leaving Antigua can browse these shops for impulsive purchases and take advantage of tax-free discounts on high-end merchandise.

Local Souvenirs & Handicrafts at Duty-Free Prices
Duty-free shopping in Antigua includes local handicrafts in addition to international brands. Numerous shops provide genuine Antiguan items, such as handcrafted jewelry and crafts as well as regionally created

souvenirs, at duty-free prices. With this special fusion of foreign and local gems, every purchase will turn into a sentimental keepsake of your trip to the Caribbean.

Plan Your Visit to Align with Significant Events

Take into account scheduling your trip to coincide with significant occasions like the Antigua and Barbuda Shopping Festival. This yearly festival features duty-free shopping along with entertainment, gastronomic treats, and cultural acts. Savor the festive mood while perusing special offers and taking in the lively vibe of the island.

Duty-Free Tobacco and Alcohol

Duty-free shopping in Antigua offers more than just clothing and accessories—it also includes pleasures like tobacco and alcohol. Take a look at the duty-free assortment of fine spirits, which includes both foreign and domestic rums. Tobacco lovers may also discover a variety of cigars and other tobacco products that come with the bonus of tax savings.

Recommendations and Booking Tips

It's important to have your passport and travel documentation available when doing duty-free shopping because these are frequently needed for tax-free purchases. To guarantee a flawless shopping experience, be informed about Antigua's and your home country's duty-free allowances. Look out for sales and discounts, particularly around holidays and celebrations.

The excitement of obtaining desired products is transformed into a tax-free journey by Antigua's duty-free shopping scene, where every transaction becomes a celebration of luxury and savings. Duty-free shopping in Antigua promises a lovely blend of leisure and retail therapy, whether you're perusing the many choices of Heritage Quay, finding locally crafted goods at duty-free prices, or indulging in luxury spirits at the airport. Thus, schedule some time for a shopping binge among the allure of the Caribbean, and allow Antigua's treasures to make a home in both your bag and your heart.

CHAPTER EIGHT

Bars and Nightclubs

Antigua comes alive with a bustling nightlife as the sun sets over the Caribbean, enticing visitors to explore the island after dark. Antigua's nightlife culture has something for everyone, from lively nightclubs thumping with music to relaxed beach bars where you can bury your toes into the sand. This is your guide to the pubs and clubs that light up the nights on this magical jewel in the Caribbean.

Shirley Heights Lookout
Shirley Heights Lookout is a popular nighttime destination as well as a daytime destination, situated atop a hill with a view of English Harbour. Locals and tourists get together for the well-known Shirley Heights Sunset Party every Sunday night. As the evening draws in, dance to the upbeat sounds of live steel drum and reggae music while taking in the expansive views of the harbor and drinking beverages. This famous location provides a laid-back and memorable beginning to Antigua's evening.

Abracadabra
Abracadabra, which is located in the center of St. John's, has long been a mainstay of Antigua's nightlife. Set to a

blend of international songs and Caribbean sounds, DJs perform a dynamic mix in this iconic nightclub. Enjoy unique drinks while dancing the night away on the outdoor dance floor or retiring to one of the comfortable lounge spaces. For a colorful and exciting night out in the capital, Abracadabra is the place to go.

Papa Zouk

Papa Zouk is a rare combination of vibrant pub and rum refuge, situated in St. John's. Renowned for its vast selection of rum, this little venue radiates Caribbean appeal with its rustic furnishings and relaxed atmosphere. Enjoy well-prepared drinks or unique rum mixes while taking in live music to create an Antiguan experience.

Coconut Grove

To enjoy a traditional Caribbean beach bar, visit Dickenson Bay's Coconut Grove. Enjoy cool beverages and live music from nearby bands while dipping your toes into the sandy sand. Coconut Grove is a favorite among residents and visitors alike because of its gorgeous beachside location and laid-back vibe, which provide the ideal balance of entertainment and relaxation.

The Crow's Nest

The Crow's Nest, a nautically themed tavern that embodies the spirit of the island's maritime past, is tucked away in ancient English Harbour. This pub offers a warm and inviting ambiance with its timber design, nautical antiques, and harbor views. Savor a variety of regional and foreign beverages while taking in the quaint settings.

Life on the Corner

Nestled in the heart of St. John's, Life on the Corner is a beloved local hangout, renowned for its genuine Caribbean atmosphere. This laid-back tavern has a varied beer menu, friendly locals, and live music. It's the perfect place to socialize with locals, take in the friendly hospitality of Antigua, and take in the laid-back nightlife of the island.

The Lime

The Lime, which is conveniently located in the center of English Harbour, provides a classy atmosphere for people looking for well-mixed drinks and unusual tastes. The wide menu at the bar offers a selection of distinctive cocktails, and skilled mixologists may make unique mixtures according to your tastes. For those seeking a sophisticated setting in which to relax, The Lime offers a chic and expensive choice.

Recommendations and Booking Tips: While some beach bars open early in the evening and night clubs stay open into the wee hours of the morning, Antigua's nightlife establishments may have different opening hours. Inspect your selected locations for any live performances, theme nights, or special events. Remember that certain places may have clothing codes, particularly in more upmarket settings.

Bars and nightclubs in Antigua provide a diverse range of activities, ranging from relaxing on the beach with your toes in the sand to dancing to reggae beats and sophisticated cocktail lounges. Antigua's nightlife welcomes you to enjoy the essence of the Caribbean after dark, whether you're dancing beneath the stars at Shirley Heights, losing yourself in the famed sounds of Abracadabra, or sipping exotic cocktails at The Lime. Thus, when the sun goes down, let the energizing energy and catchy tunes lead you to a memorable evening in this tropical paradise.

Cultural Performances of Antigua

Beyond its immaculate shores and glistening waters, Antigua enthralls tourists with a rich cultural tapestry that is brought to life via energetic performances.

Discover the rich history of the island by taking in the many cultural events that highlight Antigua's customs of storytelling, dancing, and music. Discover Antigua's captivating cultural pulse with our guide, which covers everything from tiny concerts to exuberant celebrations.

Antigua Carnival

One of the most popular celebrations in the Caribbean is Antigua Carnival, which features a spectacular display of color, music, and dancing. Every year, the carnival takes place in late July or early August and is known for its colorful street parades, exciting calypso and soca music, and masquerade bands. Come celebrate with the locals as they dress in extravagant costumes, move to catchy beats, and take part in the contagious enthusiasm that characterizes this extravagant cultural event.

Wadadli Drummers

The Wadadli Drummers are a representation of Antigua's rhythmic legacy; their name derives from the native Arawak term for the island. This vibrant trio combines African and Caribbean elements to highlight traditional Antiguan drumming. Attend their performances at festivals, cultural events, or simply beach get-togethers, where the island's history and character are echoed by the rhythmic beats.

Cultural Nights at Hotels and Resorts

Cultural nights are held in a lot of Antigua's resorts and hotels, providing a sampling of the island's artistic expressions. These nights frequently include storytelling, dancing, and music from the area, giving visitors a close-up look at Antiguan customs. Enjoying local cuisine and entertainment together creates a sensory experience that transports attendees to the island's cultural treasures.

D-Bois

Based in English Harbour, D-Bois is an Antiguan dance company that embodies the essence of Caribbean dance. D-Bois highlights the variety of Antiguan cultural expression via traditional and modern dance styles. Come see them play if you want to see how they combine storytelling, music, and dancing to capture the essence of the island.

National Youth Choir

Antigua and Barbuda's National Youth Choir is evidence of the island's vocal prowess and commitment to cultural preservation. The young vocalists in this choir present a variety of works from both domestic and foreign repertoire. Experiencing one of their concerts offers a melodic voyage across Antigua's cultural repertoire, emphasizing the ability of voice to convey the island's character.

Cultural Events

Throughout the year, Antigua has several cultural events with performances honoring the island's history. These events provide artists with a stage to display their skills, from local bands to traditional dance troupes. For an immersive experience, plan your vacation around occasions such as the Antigua and Barbuda International Literary Festival or the Green Castle Estate Mango Festival.

Antiguan Rhythm Masters

The variety of Antiguan rhythms is displayed by the Antiguan Rhythm Masters, an organization devoted to protecting and promoting the island's musical legacy. Through the use of traditional instruments and melodies in their concerts, audiences are given a chance to take in the musical fabric of the island. If you want to take a fascinating tour of Antigua's musical traditions, keep an eye out for their performances at festivals and cultural events.

Recommendations and Booking Tips

Check local event calendars and travel websites to stay up to date on forthcoming festivals and cultural events. It's best to make plans in advance for some cultural acts, as they can demand tickets or have special entrance restrictions. Talk to locals to find unannounced events or hidden treasures that aren't always obvious.

The island of Antigua may be experienced through its cultural performances, which provide a glimpse into its history, music, and dance. Every cultural event offers a new perspective on the island's history, whether you're drawn into the vibrant spectacle of Antigua Carnival, mesmerized by the National Youth Choir's melodies, or enthralled by the Wadadli Drummers' rhythmic rhythms. Allow Antigua's colorful cultural expressions to create a symphony that complements the beat of your Caribbean voyage as you tour the island.

CHAPTER NINE

Health and Safety

Making sure you are well and secure is of utmost importance when you travel to Antigua, a Caribbean treasure renowned for its sun-drenched beaches and lively culture. Visitors are made to feel quite welcome in Antigua, and with a few common sense measures, you can make the most of your time in this tropical haven. This is a thorough guide to staying safe and healthy when visiting Antigua's attractions.

Healthy Precautions
Vaccines and Health Examination: Make sure your usual immunizations are current with your healthcare professional before flying to Antigua. Although entrance does not need any special vaccines, it is essential to maintain up-to-date routine immunization records.

Mosquito Protection: Like many tropical locations, Antigua is home to mosquitoes. Use insect repellent, cover up with long sleeves and pants, and stay in lodgings with air conditioning or screens to protect yourself from mosquito-borne diseases including dengue, chikungunya, and Zika.

Sun Protection: Antigua needs sun protection precautions because of its bright atmosphere. To protect oneself from the intense Caribbean heat, wear lightweight, long-sleeved clothes, sunglasses, a hat, and sunscreen with a high SPF.

Food and Water Safety

Water in bottles: Although Antigua's tap water is usually safe to drink, many tourists would rather use bottled water. It's easily accessible, and using it to wash your teeth and drink might help you feel more at ease.

Keeping Food Clean: Savoring the regional food is a vacation highlight. Eat only at respectable establishments, and make sure the seafood is cooked correctly and fresh. It is advisable to wash or peel fruits and vegetables before eating them, and only eat food from street sellers that has been prepared and served hot.

Medical Facilities

Quality of Healthcare: Medical facilities in Antigua are well-equipped; one such facility is the Mount St. John's Medical Centre located in St. John's. There are several private medical facilities on the island. Even if there is medical care accessible, it is imperative to get travel insurance that includes evacuation and emergency medical coverage.

Medicines: Major towns have pharmacies where you may get over-the-counter drugs for common illnesses. But it's a good idea to include any special prescriptions you might require for your vacation.

Guides for Safety:
Crime Precautions: Although Antigua is usually seen to be secure, it's advisable to use caution when traveling anywhere. Use hotel safes to store your valuables, avoid flaunting them in public, and use caution while venturing into new places, particularly after midnight.

Safety in Transportation: Put safety first whether you're taking public transit, hiring a car, or utilizing a cab. Pay attention to traffic laws in your area, buckle up, and drive carefully, especially on curves.

Safety in Water: Make sure operators have the required credentials and adhere to safety protocols if you intend to participate in water sports. Pay attention to lifeguard warnings on beaches and use caution near strong currents.

Medical Procedures: Observe any established health precautions, such as mask use and social separation. To keep yourself and the neighborhood safe, abide by the local rules.

Emergency Services: To get help right away in an emergency, contact 911.

Embassy or Consulate: Be aware of the phone number and email address of your nation's embassy or consulate in Antigua so that you may get help in case something goes wrong.

You may make sure that your trip to Antigua is safe and enjoyable by following these easy steps. Traveling with health and safety in mind will allow you to enjoy the rich cultural diversity of the island, see its natural beauty, and embrace the warmth of Caribbean hospitality. Happy exploring and have a safe trip!

Communication

Keeping in touch is crucial for a flawless and pleasurable trip to Antigua, a Caribbean paradise of sun-drenched beaches and lively culture. Here is your entire guide to communication in Antigua, covering everything from appreciating cultural subtleties to navigating local communication networks.

Mobile Network Accessibility

Local SIM Cards: Think about getting a local SIM card when you get there for an affordable local connection. The two biggest mobile service providers in Antigua are Digicel and Flow; they sell data plans for cell phones along with prepaid SIM cards.

Coverage: Most major towns and populous areas have dependable mobile coverage. However, signal strength may differ in more isolated or hilly areas.

Online Connectivity
Accessibility of WiFi: The majority of Antigua's resorts, hotels, and cafés have Wi-Fi available. For information on Wi-Fi availability and any related fees, get in touch with your lodging.

Web cafes: Major cities provide internet cafés as an option for online access if you don't have a mobile data package. Because the rates are typically fair, staying in touch is convenient.

Dialing codes and Local Calls
Local Calls: It's simple to make local calls. To make a call within Antigua, just dial the seven-digit local number. When making an international call, dial the desired number first, then the country code.

Calls for emergencies: In Antigua, 911 is the emergency number for law enforcement, fire departments, and ambulances. Keep this number handy for easy access to help in an emergency.

Tips for Cultural Communication
Welcoming Traditions: People from Antigua are renowned for being hospitable and kind. When entering a location, a basic "good morning" or "good afternoon" is customary. Being nice and having friendly chats is greatly appreciated.

Complimentary Phrases: Antigua's national language is English, and the people there value courteous and courteous communication. Say "please" and "thank you" to show consideration, and greet individuals using titles like Mr., Mrs., or Miss.

3. Island Time: Antigua follows a loose schedule that is commonly known as "island time." Recognize that scheduled schedules for meetings and services might not always be precisely followed. Accept the relaxed vibe and give yourself leeway while making arrangements.

Communication in Public Transportation
Transportation: In Antigua, taxis are widely available. Before you leave, ask the driver to confirm the fare.

Sharing cabs with other patrons is a popular practice that lowers expenses.

Buses: Antigua has a non-formal yet efficient bus system. Buses might not follow set timetables, so find out the routes and times by asking about or at bus stations.

Managing Linguistic differences
Dialects in English: Even though English is the official language, certain Antiguans may have an accent or dialect. Asking for clarification is always acceptable if you run across any linguistic quirks.

Cultural Sensitivity: Be mindful of cultural variances and receptive to discovering more about Antigua's rich past. Talk to people, hear their experiences, and appreciate the diversity of the island's cultures.

Traveling Abroad:
Check with Your Provider: If you want to use the mobile number from your home country, inquire about international roaming capabilities and related costs from your service provider.

Roaming Data: Use caution when roaming your data to prevent unforeseen fees. When performing data-intensive tasks, connect to Wi-Fi whenever feasible.

Efficient communication makes a big difference in Antigua, whether you're seeing historical sites, shopping, or just relaxing on the beach. Accept the welcoming environment of the island, maintain connections with locals, and value the subtle cultural differences that make communicating in Antigua a fun part of your Caribbean vacation. Happy exploration and safe travels!

Local Etiquette

Understanding and adopting local etiquette enhances your experience and promotes pleasant encounters with the kind Antiguan people as you enter the sun-kissed embrace of Antigua, renowned for its immaculate beaches and colorful culture. This is your handbook to the subtleties of regional manners, which will aid you in navigating the social seas of this idyllic Caribbean location.

Salutations and Etiquette
Warm regards: People from Antigua are known for being hospitable and kind. When passing someone on the street or entering a venue, a brief "good morning" or "good afternoon" is a polite and common greeting.

The Importance of Politeness In Antigua, politeness is highly regarded. Sayings like "please" and "thank you" are essential components of polite conversation and not merely formalities.

Time on the Island
Appreciate Lazy Schedules: Antigua follows "island time," which is a more relaxed schedule. It's possible that meetings and services won't always begin or conclude on time, so adjust your schedule accordingly and accept the casual pace.

The Virtue of Patience Patience is essential, whether you're waiting in line for public transit or a dinner at a neighborhood eatery. People from Antigua value composure and empathy.

Respectful Conduct
Honoring Elders: When addressing senior citizens, use titles such as Mr., Mrs., or Miss out of respect. This is regarded as courteous and shows cultural sensitivity.

Classic Clothes: Even though Antigua has a relaxed vibe, it is respectful to dress modestly, especially when visiting local villages or places of worship.

Awareness of Cultures

Involve and Acquire: Antigua is a cultural melting pot where you may discover more about the island's rich past by interacting with its people. Ask questions, pay attention to the stories, and demonstrate a sincere interest in the customs and traditions.

Recognizing Diversities: The people of Antigua hail from many cultural origins, and the island values cultural plurality. Remain receptive and refrain from concluding outward appearances.

Reception Manners
Wait to Be Seated: Avoid selecting your table at restaurants; instead, wait to be seated by the staff. This shows respect for the institution and is standard procedure.

Expressing Grace: Many Antiguan homes have a tradition of saying grace before meals. Participating in this activity is a considerate show of support if you are welcomed to a local residence.

Customs of Tipping
Congratulations: In Antigua, it is traditional to tip, and certain establishments may add a service fee to your bill. If not, a gratuity of around 10% to 15% would be appreciated.

Acknowledgment of Services: Thanking waiters, in hotels or restaurants, is a little but important part of regional manners.

Interaction with Others
Casual Conversations: Whether in a market, on the beach, or at a store, strike up a casual discussion with the locals. People from Antigua are amiable and love mingling with guests.

Private Area: Although most Antiguans are kind and hospitable, it's still necessary to respect people's personal space. Recognize that cultural norms about physical touch differ.

Respect for the Environment
Appreciation of Nature: The people of Antigua are proud of their natural surroundings. By abstaining from littering and being aware of your environmental effects, you can support the island's sustainability efforts.

Actions for Conservation: Antigua participates significantly in environmental initiatives. Encourage eco-friendly behaviors and programs that help protect the island's scenic beauty.

You may easily navigate Antigua's social scene and create lasting relationships with the friendly locals by implementing these elements of local etiquette into your encounters. Your adherence to local etiquette becomes an essential part of the spectacular experiences that await you in this Caribbean haven as you enjoy the rich culture and unique heritage of Antigua. Enjoy your journey into Antigua's heart, where friendly smiles and respect for cultural differences open doors to an incredibly rewarding experience.

CONCLUSION

Upon bidding adieu to Antigua's sun-kissed coastlines, the memories woven throughout your Caribbean vacation create a magical fabric that surpasses everyday life. Beyond its immaculate beaches and crystal-clear waters, Antigua captivates with a symphony of cultural diversity, friendly locals, and beautiful scenery that stays with you long after your trip is over.

The pace of life pulses to the cadence of laughing, the vivid colors of carnival festivities, and the melodies of reggae resonating against ancient ports in this oasis of sun-soaked happiness. The kind welcome of Antiguans and their dedication to protecting a rich cultural legacy foster an environment that makes the island seem like a home away from home.

Antigua's diverse appeal gradually reveals itself, from the excitement of touring historical monuments and delighting in lively local markets to the peaceful times spent on isolated beaches. A unique balance of excitement and relaxation is created on the island by the combination of contemporary conveniences and island time, where the sunsets signal the start of a vibrant nightlife.

Antigua is more than simply a place to visit; it's an entire experience that connects with the natural rhythms of the area and the genuineness of its inhabitants. The island's dedication to sustainable development and environmental preservation is a reflection of its strong bond with the immaculate landscapes that turn every bend into a picture-perfect setting.

Antigua is like a masterpiece in the fabric of travel experiences, with every element adding to the overall charm. Antigua invites visitors to fully immerse themselves, whether it's in sampling the delicacies of regional cuisine, dancing beneath the stars at Shirley Heights, or learning about the subtle cultural differences that define the island's uniqueness.

Antigua's unique beauty is found not only in its spectacular landscapes but also in the intangible moments that etch themselves into your soul. Keep this in mind as you carry the sounds of steel drum music, the warmth of the Caribbean sun, and the genuine smiles of the people. The locations you've seen, the relationships you've made, the tales you've heard, and the lively spirit that has become a part of your journey are all examples of Antigua's lasting influence.

Antigua is more than simply a place to visit; it's an incredible experience that beckons you to discover more of its charm at every turn. It's the promise of orange and pink sunsets, the sound of palm trees rustling in the wind, and the ageless charm of a Caribbean paradise that beckons you back to surrender to its alluring embrace.

Printed in Great Britain
by Amazon